SPATTER PATTERN

PATTERN

or,
How I Got Away With It

Neal Bell

BROADWAY PLAY PUBLISHING INC
224 E 62nd St, NY, NY 10065
www.broadwayplaypub.com
info@broadwayplaypub.com

First printing: May 2006
I S B N: 0-88145-292-0

Book design: Marie Donovan
Word processing: Microsoft Word
Typographic controls: Ventura Publisher
Typeface: Palatino
Printed and bound in the U S A

SPATTER PATTERN was first performed at
Playwrights Horizons (Tim Sanford, Artistic Director)
on 30 September 2004. The cast and creative
contributors were:

DUNN . . . . .Peter Frechette
TATE . . . . Darren Pettie
ACTRESS . . . . Deirdre O'Connell
ACTOR . . . . .John Lavelle

Director . . . . .Michael Greif
Sets . . . . Mark Wendland
Costumes . . . . Miranda Hoffman
Lighting . . . . .Kevin Adams
Sound . . . . .Jill B C DuBoff
Music . . . . Michael Friedman
Production stage manager . . . . .Judith Schoenfeld

CHARACTERS & SETTING

DUNN, *a writer, early fifties*

TATE, *a college professor, mid-forties*

ACTRESS *plays:*
SELMA, *an agent*
ELLEN, TATE's *wife*
MS FISHER, *a mortuary employee*
MRS ROTH, *an elderly woman*
ANDREA, *a college student*
HOOKER

ACTOR *plays:*
REALTOR
DETECTIVE
MANCHESKI, *a college student*
MOXLEY, *a funeral parlor salesman*
HUSTLER

The present

New York City

TWO NOTES

All scenic elements mentioned in stage directions—
windows, doors, walls, beds, etc—are meant to be suggested.
Not literal.

In scenes from DUNN'*s point of view,* DUNN *will sometimes*
"edit" the conversation, playing it out a different way in his
mind. When he returns to "reality"—or to another edited
version—this will be indicated by the stage direction,
"We go back..."

Scene One

(Central Park. DUNN *and his agent* SELMA *are having a "business lunch".*
SELMA*'s sprung for hot-dogs, which they're eating while they talk.)*

SELMA: *(Holding up a manuscript)* So you thought this would be commercial—

DUNN: I wasn't thinking—

SELMA: No, I got that part.

DUNN: —about what you'd do with it.

SELMA: *(Agreeing that* DUNN*'s been thoughtless)* How I could sell it.

DUNN: I just wanted to—write, something.

SELMA: Like therapy.

DUNN: Maybe.

SELMA: I'm supposed to market your therapy. I smell Oscar!

DUNN: If you don't like it, you could just say—

SELMA: I don't like it. A lot. What is it?

DUNN: A love-story...

SELMA: With lepers. Actual non-metaphorical lepers.

DUNN: *One* leper.

SELMA: "...and the woman who loves him."

DUNN: All right, it sounds dumb when you put it like that.

SELMA: And why a woman? Couldn't it be two guys, living, loving, croaking?

DUNN: I wasn't sure who'd want to see a movie about gay lepers.

(*Pause*)

SELMA: Whereas the niche for a straight-couple leper romance...

DUNN: Let me have my script.

(SELMA *hands it to him.*)

SELMA: I'm sorry David died.
I'm sorry you can't seem to get it together.

DUNN: You're letting me go?

SELMA: I oughta. But you're a challenge:
how the fuck do I sell you?
 (*Pause*)
C'mon—you've been with us way too long.
And you mean too much to the agency...
(*Getting choked up*)
And to me—and if you ever tell a living soul I was crying—...

(*Now we go back, to the actual [dry-eyed] end of the conversation.*)

DUNN: You're letting me go?

SELMA: What can I say? Ten percent of nothing is nada.
(*Pause*)
And the wiener's two bucks.

DUNN: This isn't a business lunch?

(SELMA *looks askance.*)

DUNN: I'll send you a check.

(*Discouraged, he walks off, passing* TATE, *a slightly younger man, who's out for a walk.*)

(SELMA *stares at* TATE, *astonished.*)

SELMA: Oh my god —it's you!

TATE: I don't think so.

(*Enchanted,* SELMA *blocks his way.*)

SELMA: No, I mean you're him.

TATE: I'm not.
People keep mistaking me for the guy,
and it's getting tedious:
I can't even go for a walk in the park—

SELMA: Do you have an agent?

TATE: What?

SELMA: You gotta have somebody selling your
story—right?

TATE: No. And I don't want—

SELMA: You don't know what you want! Until you want
it.
Let me give you my card—

(*She whips out a card, he takes it.*)

SELMA: The name is—

TATE: (*Glancing at the card*)
Selma, listen carefully: if you say another word,
I'll have to snap your neck like a twig.

SELMA: (*Seeing he's serious*)
There are people around!

TATE: There were people around before...

(*He moves off—*SELMA *watches him go, shaken but seeing
dollar signs.*)

(*The lights change.*)

Scene Two

(DUNN *and the* REALTOR *are looking at an apartment.*)

DUNN: It's small.

REALTOR: It's the City. This is a palace.
You should see where I live, it's a closet.

DUNN: Studio?

REALTOR: No. A closet in a studio. I'm subletting.

(DUNN *moves into the room.*)

REALTOR: So whaddya think?
(*Pause*)
Take your time.
(*Pause*) I got other clients.
(*Pause*)
Whaddya think?

DUNN: Neighbors?

REALTOR: What about 'em?

DUNN: Loud?

REALTOR: I don't hear anything.

DUNN: They're at work.
Or they're dead.

(*The* REALTOR *eyes* DUNN.)

DUNN: Do you ever sit in your—closet?
Truly, a closet?—

REALTOR: (*Shrugs*) It's a walk-in.

DUNN: —and you wait for your neighbors' usual
late-night screaming-match...but it never comes...
All you can hear is a soft wet sound, like something
running down a splayed arm and seeping into the

carpet...
Maybe, way far off, an ambulance dying away.
And then nothing.

(The conversation goes back, picks up:)

DUNN: Neighbors?

REALTOR: What about 'em?

DUNN: Loud?

REALTOR: I don't hear anything.

DUNN: They're at work.

(Pause)

REALTOR: Tell ya what—
pick up a key at the office tonight, I'm always around.
(Pause)
Where else would I be?
Not having a life:
opening doors into empty rooms...
(Echoing)
"...Hello?...hello?..."

(We go back:)

REALTOR: Tell ya what, pick up a key at the office
tonight.
I'm always around.
Come back here and let yourself in,
you can stay as long as you want to.
But like I said, pre-war, the walls are solid, you won't
hear a lot...somebody banging a pot on the stove, I
dunno, *I Love Lucy* re-runs...

(DUNN looks out a window.)

DUNN: That's south?

REALTOR: Yep. *(Pause)* You gay?

DUNN: *(Acknowledging)* Mmmph...

REALTOR: Single?

DUNN: No. I've got an invisible boyfriend.

(Pause)

REALTOR: Widower? Still haunted by the past?
"Gone are the days..."

DUNN: *(Lost)* A lot of days—twenty-three years.
"Start your life over again!" No problem.

(We go back:)

REALTOR: You gay?

DUNN: Mmmph...

REALTOR: Single?

DUNN: Why?

REALTOR: I could tell you about the neighborhood.

DUNN: I can probably figure it out. If I take the place.
I will come back tonight.

REALTOR: O-kay. You've seen enough, for now?

(DUNN nods, REALTOR checks his list.)

REALTOR: Then we hop in a cab to Tribeca.
(He moves them out the door, into the hallway.)
One bedroom, onto an airshaft,
but it's bigger than this, if you don't mind living in
twilight all day long...

*(DUNN pauses to make a note on his list of apartments.
The REALTOR tries to hide his impatience.)*

REALTOR: Mister Dunn—

(DUNN doesn't hear him.)

REALTOR: Take your time. I'll get the elevator.

*(The REALTOR exits. DUNN finishes up, then looks around.
He approaches another [unseen] door, reads the name-plate.)*

DUNN: "Mrs Sylvia Roth."

REALTOR: Old lady with multiple cats, would be my guess.
You ready to roll?

(DUNN *approaches the [unseen] door on the other side.*)

DUNN: "M Tate." Why does that name ring a—

(*The offstage elevator dings.* DUNN *calls out, to the* REALTOR:)

DUNN: "M Tate." Mean anything to you?

REALTOR: (*Off*) O K, you're coming from Yonkers,
so this'll boggle your suburban mind:
but millions of people live here—
and most of them will spend their whole lives without
knowing that you existed.
Give yourself a few months, you'll be just as ignorant.
You have to be.

(*We go back:*)

DUNN: ...Why does that name ring a—

(*Elevator dings.* DUNN *calls out:*)

DUNN: "M Tate"?Mean anything to you?

REALTOR: (*Off*) Elevator!

Scene Three

(*An interrogation room
A* HOMICIDE DETECTIVE *is questioning* TATE.)

TATE: I've been over this! Jesus. How many times...

DETECTIVE: But not with me. I'm the new guy.
Maybe a fresh pair of eyes, they were thinkin'...

TATE: *(In the middle of a thought)*
Then *you* tell me why they never found any blood on
my clothes—...

DETECTIVE: Because you're standing behind her.
(He demonstrates, grabbing TATE *in a half nelson.)*
Right-handed?

TATE: *(Choking)* Yes.

DETECTIVE: Like this, then.

(He "slashes" TATE'*s throat, with the side of his hand.)*

TATE: And no blood on the sleeve of my coat, because...?
My arm is right there, in the path of the
spatter-pattern—

DETECTIVE: "Spatter-pattern?"

TATE: I'm sawing my way through her neck—

DETECTIVE: "Spatter pattern." Huh.

TATE: I watch T V.

(Pause. The DETECTIVE *lets* TATE *go.)*

DETECTIVE: You didn't saw through her neck:
c'mon, like an old tin can and a Ginzu knife?
"And still it can cut a slice of tomato this thin!..."
So you had, like a boxcutter? What?
(Pause)
So you had, I don't know, like a thing for her? What?
(Pause)
Isn't that, strictly speaking, something you aren't
supposed to do?
Fuck your students?
"In loco parentis", and all—
which, O K, in the Ozarks maybe
is porking the young'uns...
so then, I guess, you could, too—in his place—
except we're not in the Ozarks, bucko.
And here, 'in loco parentis' means—

TATE: I know what it means.

DETECTIVE: Right—I forget:
you're an educated man.

(*Pause*)

TATE: I didn't "pork" any young'uns.
I didn't fuck this student.
I didn't follow her home, that night.

DETECTIVE: She never got home.
You killed her.
(*Pause*)
She wasn't raped, she wasn't robbed.
She was just snuffed out.
It was personal.

TATE: For what I wish was the final time: are you
charging me?

DETECTIVE: Not now.

TATE: But you plan to keep dragging me down here...

DETECTIVE: Your wife wouldn't give you an alibi,
because...?

TATE: ... of her high regard for the truth?
I *wasn't* home that night.
I could've been, watching the fucking Iron Chef.
But they got to the squid sorbet,
and that's when I
made the worst decision of my life—
I went for a walk.

DETECTIVE: Three hours. And no one saw you.

TATE: Isn't that the whole point of New York?

(*Pause*)

DETECTIVE: (*Studying his file*)
You were in the Middle East...

TATE: And Sheboygan. And Ulan Bator. I've traveled.
So far, nothing beats Disneyland.

DETECTIVE: ...around the start of the first Gulf War.

TATE: Right out of the Navy—yes:
I ended up in the diplomatic corps.

DETECTIVE: You gotta know the rumor on
campus—you were some kind of Special Op.

TATE: My students, some of them, also believe
Homer Simpson was running for President.

DETECTIVE: You kill anyone in Iraq?
(Pause)
Just wondering. War-time. Not the same,
I know. As slitting a woman's throat
in peacetime, on a street in Manhattan.
A woman who happened to be a student of yours,
but—just a coincidence.
With friends who say you might have been harassing
her—

TATE: Which is ridiculous.

DETECTIVE: —and that she was angry because you
weren't doing your job, as her advisor.
Professor Tate—in the alley—with the knife:
whaddya think?
*(Again he makes the "slashing the throat" gesture,
into the air.)*
A short, serrated blade, is what we're looking for.
Like a K-bar.
Like a Navy SEAL would use—
basic weapon, right? For a Special Op?

TATE: I didn't kill Andrea Evans.
(Pause)
Or sleep with her, or do anything except try to open her
mind.

DETECTIVE: Well, it's open now, wide: the worms crawl in, the worms crawl out.

(TATE *stares at him.*)

DETECTIVE: You're free to go, Mister Tate.

TATE: I don't think I'm free to do anything.
(Pause)
What would it take, to get you off my back?

DETECTIVE: I dunno—an alibi?
(Pause)
Or find us a better suspect.

(The lights change.)

Scene Four

(DUNN, *using a pass-key, opens the door to the empty apartment.*
He steps inside, closes the door behind him. Stands, listens...
We can hear somebody coughing.
Then the wail of a distant ambulance
The fifties sound of the I Love Lucy *show comes floating in.*
DUNN *goes to a window, stares out at the night.*
TATE *enters the hall, crosses to his apartment door, lets himself in*
He closes and locks the door. Tired, he pulls up a chair, sits down.
He starts crying—softly at first, and then more audibly. He's shaken.
DUNN *hears the crying next door. He takes a step closer to the [invisible] dividing wall.*
The other sounds of the night fade away.
TATE's *crying is more noticeable, in the silence.*
DUNN *listens. Then he takes out his cell-phone, punches in a number.)*

DUNN: (*Into phone*) Mister Kravitz? It's Edward Dunn—
Is that place we saw in Tribeca still—
(...)
It's not. O K. How about the garden apartment in
Park—
(...)
Gone.
(...)
No, I'm there right now.
(...)
Well, it's not exactly a cork-lined room—
(...)
That's right. Ever read any Proust?
(...)
No, me neither. High on my list—
which is growing ever longer:
Things I Want To Do Some Day,
Knowing I Never Will.

(*In the next room,* TATE *gets up, approaches an [unseen] C D
player, puts on a C D—the quiet second movement of Ravel's*
Piano Concerto in G—*starts it up, sits down again.*)

DUNN: (...)
"Sky-diving"? Maybe. I always wanted to fly,
except—you're not really flying, you're falling.
(...)
"The glass is half-empty." That's right.
Not even half. I broke the glass.
(...)
"Getting married?" That one I did—
a version of that—advanced sky-diving:
"Up in the sky—it's a bird, it's a plane, it's—
no—*two* birds, *two* planes—
splatt."
You hit the ground hard.
And one of you hits the ground first.

(*We go back:*)

DUNN: "Getting married?" That one I did—
a version of that—
(...)
No, *he* was the woman.

(We go back:)

DUNN: No, we were both men—
(...)
But it's about more than plumbing, Mister Kravitz...

(We go back:)

DUNN: "Getting married?" That one I did—
a version of that—I had a companion...
(...)
Twenty-three years.
(...)
No, not AIDS.
My people often die of something else.
Like other people.
I don't mean we die *of* other people—
well, sometimes we do, Matthew Shepard—
but, by and large, if we stay in our ghettoes,
being avid consumers, pumping our ill-gotten gains
into the bloated permanent-war economy...

(We go back:)

DUNN: —a version of that—I had a companion...

(Now TATE *re-enters his room, a bottle of beer in hand, and
smoking a cigarette. He sits and listens to the music.)*

DUNN: Almost half of my life. He died.
Lung cancer. He was a smoker.
He was a drinker. He was an asshole.
(...)
I know: I lived with an asshole twenty-three years.
What does that say about me?
(...)
No, I'm not crying, it's just—

the guy in the next apartment is playing—
(...)
—not our song, our song was *I'm In You,*
Peter Frampton—how scary is that?
This is something classical. Slow.
(...)
Not loud. I can barely hear it.
In fact, it may not be there at all.
(Pause)
Sometimes I think I hear David, in the next room,
and just for a second...

(We go back:)

DUNN: Not loud. I can barely hear it.
You were right, about the walls.
So—in the time I've been talking to you,
no one's taken this place?
(...)
Then I want it.

(The lights change.)

Scene Five

(A lecture-hall. TATE is finishing up a class.)

TATE: So the topic of your next assignment will be
"political courage." And—whoever you write about—
pick someone whose battle you can identify with:
what frightens *you*? The war, for example—
would you have voted against it? Knowing that vote
would probably sabotage your career?
(Pause)
I've told you more than you care to know,
about my service days, in the Gulf.
But I never told you about one night—
a moonless night, off the coast of Kuwait,
we're in the water, doing a recon—

then, behind us, out in the Gulf, the U S S *Princeton* hit a
mine...
There was a flash of light, and a sound
I didn't hear, I *felt*—like a blow.
And my hands started shaking.
I couldn't stop them.
I dropped the plastic slate—where I was
recording the depth of the water—
crucial information, if the Marines had to
storm the beach. But I was afraid.
I dropped the slate. And it sank down into the dark.
(Pause)
Why was I there? Why had I gone to war?
Because I was brave? Or because I'd been afraid—
all my life—
that I wasn't?
(Pause)
"Will this be on the test?"
No. But whatever you write about, look
for the motive under the motive. Clear? Questions?
(Pause)
Signs of life? Pulse?
Is— *(Consults a seating-chart)* —Mister Mancheski
snoring?

(The student, MANCHESKI*—disheveled—stands up in the
audience.)*

MANCHESKI: I was awake. I swear.
I caught up on my sleep in Rocks For Jocks.

TATE: It's quieter?

MANCHESKI: I sit further back.

TATE: And now, refreshed, you were thinking...

MANCHESKI: About being afraid. Like you said.
I'm afraid of myself. Because—things bother me.
And I get so angry, sometimes, that I think—
...like cell-phones! And they're everywhere!

"I have always depended upon the kindness of—"
RING!
And the woman answers it!
"Hi—I'm at a play—
Streetcar—really bad, but it's almost over,
they're dragging her off, right now..."
AM I ALONE?

TATE: Mister Mancheski—

MANCHESKI: *(Ignoring)* In the universe? Am I?
I think—sometimes—I'm so alone—that
I could kill somebody.

TATE: We're beyond inappropriate, Mister Mancheski—
meaning, class dismissed—

(Near MANCHESKI, *a cell-phone starts to ring.)*

TATE: Oh Jesus—

MANCHESKI: What is that fucking song?

TATE: It's *Fur Elise.*

MANCHESKI: Then why doesn't she answer it?
At this funeral I went to,
"Dust to dust, ashes to—" RING!
"The peace that passes all—" RING!
"Oh, hi—at Andrea's funeral—
really sad, but it's almost over..."

TATE: *(Reacting to Andrea's name)* Mr. Mancheski.
Everyone is gone.
Could the phone be yours?

*(*MANCHESKI *roots through his backpack, digs out a
phone—it's ringing:* Fur Elise.)

MANCHESKI: *(Answering)* Hello?
(...)
Yeah, I'll ask him.
(...)
Not a problem. Later.

(He hangs up.)
Much later, I hope.
That was her.

TATE: That was who?

MANCHESKI: Your late student—Andrea Evans.
Wanted to know if you sleep at night.

(Pause)

TATE: Get out of here.

MANCHESKI: I wanta know, too.
Because—I was almost in love with her.
Maybe I would have gotten there.
If you had let her live.

(Pause)

TATE: This isn't working, is it?
Why did I think I could go on teaching?

MANCHESKI: My question would be—
why hasn't the university
fired your ass?

(Pause)

TATE: If I didn't kill her, Mister Mancheski—
who did? A total stranger. Why not?
Because you don't want the world to work that way?

MANCHESKI: Professor Tate?

TATE: What?

MANCHESKI: Your hands are shaking.

(He makes the sound of a mine exploding. TATE *glares at him.)*

(The lights change.)

Scene Six

(DUNN *is at home, at his computer, trying to write.*
He speaks his words, as he types.)

DUNN: "For a...long time...I would...go to bed...early...
Sometimes...the candle...barely out..."
(*He stops, smacks his forehead.*)
No. *Commercial!* Moron.
(*He shakes his head:*)
Proust. C'mon, Marcel, get out of bed!, for crying out
loud...
(*He tries again, starts typing:*)
"Last night I...dreamt...I went to...Manderly—"
(*He stops.*)
Better...

(*He starts again:*)

DUNN: "Last night I dreamt that David and I were on a
train to New Haven—"
(*He stops, deletes, retypes:*)
"...a train to Paris...and I knew he was dead—
(*He stops, deletes, retypes:*)
"...knew that he was sick, but that was O K,
because there was a wonderful doctor in Paris,
a miracle-worker..."
(*He stops, thinks, starts typing again.*)

(*Lights fade on* DUNN, *up on* TATE, *who's in his former*
apartment, watching ELLEN, *his wife, as she packs a bag.*)

TATE: You could have told the police I was with you.

ELLEN: No—I rolled over, and I distinctly remember:
you weren't there.
(*Pause*)
I slept with a student once.

TATE: Please—

ELLEN: I think you need to hear this.

TATE: And I can swear, with almost absolute certainty,
that I don't.

ELLEN: When you were away, on your "mission to
Iraq"—
whatever that was....
He smelled like you did once, back in the day—
like a big wet dog.
(*Pause*)
I lied to you. About that boy.

TATE: And now you don't trust *me*?

(*Pause*)

ELLEN: You have to tell me—once and for all—
did you hurt that girl?

TATE: No.

ELLEN: No, you didn't? Or no, you won't tell me.

TATE: No, it doesn't matter. (*Pause*) I've been fired.

ELLEN: (*Genuinely surprised*) I don't blame them—*I*
would have canned you.
But is that legal?
You haven't even been charged.

TATE: I'm notorious.
Making it hard, they said, for my students
to concentrate in my class.
Which, of course, assumes they ever did—
but I guess that's moot.
I've already moved out. Now you're selling our home.
What do I have left?
So whether I fucked this girl, or I didn't—
or even whether I killed her or not—
it doesn't matter because, as far as the world is
concerned, I'm guilty.

I almost wish I was. Then I could do anything.
I'd be free.

(ELLEN, *disconcerted, returns to furious packing.*)

(TATE *approaches her from behind.*)

ELLEN: (*Trying to ignore him*)
If you didn't kill her—who did?

(TATE *puts his hands on her shoulders. She shudders but
doesn't move.*)

TATE: It's a poser. I was thinking you.

(*She listens to him, appalled but fascinated.*)

TATE: Because you were getting old.
Because you thought I was fucking around.
Because *you* fucked around—to get even with me—
and only got lonelier.
Because you used to stand outside my office,
with your ear to the door—
and there were times when you didn't hear a thing,
and you'd remember how, when I went down on you,
you were quiet, biting your lip, not making a sound,
like you didn't want me to know what I was doing to
you...

(*He makes the sound of his wife's low moan, she flinches.*)

TATE: This student you were jealous of—Ms Andrea
Evans—
the dead one?
She was comparing America, today, to Nazi Germany.
I told her—to her great irritation—
I found her analogies facile.
I'd explain why—
and she'd think about it. In silence.
Ellen, that's all you heard:
a silence you couldn't understand.
So you found a knife—the one I thought I'd lost,

from my days in the service—
and you stood in the dark of an alley,
wondering how your life had come down to this—
and when my student walked by, you grabbed her.
And opened her up to the elements.

(She pulls away from him, hesitates.)

ELLEN: None of that happened.

TATE: Prove it.

(Pause. She slaps him hard.)

ELLEN: Find another victim.
(Grabbing her overstuffed suitcase, she exits.)

*(TATE watches her go. Lights stay on TATE, come up on
DUNN, who's reading a print-out of what he wrote.)*

DUNN: "And the doctor in Paris was saying,
'A year...maybe six months...'"

(Pause. DUNN chides himself:)

DUNN: Not dying. Nobody's sick-room. Murder. Sex.
Commercial. Moron.
(He starts typing again, speaking as he types:)
"...And the doctor in Paris—tres jolie, though he
smelled like he hadn't bathed in a week—was saying,
'It's just a pulled muscle, my friend.
What did you think it was?'"

(The lights change.)

Scene Seven

*(DUNN's bedroom, in the new apartment. Late at night
(DUNN has fallen asleep, in his clothes. He's
restless—having a very bad dream.
In the next apartment, TATE staggers in. He's drunk.
He comes into his bedroom.*

Seething, he kicks out at a chair, loudly knocking it over.
DUNN *wakes up, with a start.*
For a moment he doesn't know where he is.)

DUNN: David...?

(A curtain at the [unseen] window stirs in the breeze.
DUNN *realizes no one is there.)*

DUNN: No.
(He settles back in bed, staring up at the dark.)

*(*TATE, *in his bedroom, stumbles around as he tries to take off his clothes.*
A portable phone by his bed starts ringing.
DUNN, *hearing it faintly, turns to look at the [unseen] wall.*
TATE *checks his watch.)*

TATE: Three o'clock in the fucking A M, who the fuck—
unless—
(He picks up the phone.)
Ellen?
Who is this? Hello?...Hello?
(No one at the other end. He clicks the phone off, drops it, continues undressing.)

*(*DUNN *is falling asleep again.*
TATE's *down to his underwear when the phone starts ringing again.*
Grim, he picks it up. This time he feels a presence at the other end.)

TATE: Look—this isn't you—because you're dead—
so whoever the fuck you are—
I'm not afraid. I can prove it.
You wanta hear my heart? Hold on...
(He struggles out of his T-shirt, holds the phone to his chest.)
Slow, steady, strong...
(He puts the phone back to his ear.)
You wanta hear my cock?
(He drops his boxers, stands in the nude, holding the phone to

his crotch.)
Also strong, steady, long—
but not much for conversation...
(He puts the phone back to his ear.)
My cock has nothing to say, at present.
So if I can speak for it:
(He shouts—as if he were coming, holding the phone very close.)
HUNH! HUNH!

(As TATE *throws the phone away,* DUNN *sits up again, startled, looking around.)*

DUNN: David? Is that you?

*(*TATE's *shouting fades to a mutter, as he stumbles to the door.)*

TATE: By which I mean...by which I mean—fuck *you!*
The dead stay dead.
That's a quote—from her—which you'd know,
if you read the affidavits...

*(*DUNN *strains to hear more—but there's nothing.* TATE *has exited.*
Afraid he'll never get back to sleep now, DUNN *sits up.)*

DUNN: *(To the unseen David)*
David...
When I try to see your face, in my mind...
just a blur.
Like you were being erased.
How many different ways can you leave me behind?
Get sick, get dead, disappear...
When I try to see your face—

(Suddenly there's a blast of heavy metal from TATE's *apartment.)*

DUNN: *(Barely audible above the head-banging)*
No. Absolutely not. Oh no...
(He jumps out of bed, grabs a shoe and starts pounding on

the [unseen] wall, yelling to the rhythm of his bangs:)
Thanks for waking me UP,
I'd fallen asleep in my clothes
like a homeless person,
like the guy in the subway today,
who shouted, "I don't wanta hurt anyone."
Which made us all feel better—
(Stops banging a moment)
—assuming he meant it.
Maybe he didn't...
(Starts banging again with his shoe)
Turn your stereo DOWN,
you son of a bitch,
I don't wanta hurt anyone...
(He slumps on his bed, stymied.)
Or maybe I do...

(The music plays on. DUNN shouts over it:)

DUNN: HOW MANY DIFFERENT WAYS CAN YOU
LEAVE ME BEHIND!

(There's a momentary silence.)

DUNN: Like I left you...
(As it hits him:)
Oh Jesus... did I ever pick you up?

(The music roars again.)

(The lights change.)

Scene Eight

*(DUNN is in a funeral parlor, talking to MR MOXLEY, one of
the salesmen.)*

MOXLEY: It's possible we don't have them.

DUNN: Excuse me?

MOXLEY: Mister Dunn, you signed a contract—
stating that you would pick up the cremains of your
friend—

DUNN: O K—I'm sorry, but is 'cremains' a word?
I don't think it is.

MOXLEY: It means "cremated remains"—

DUNN: Then, if you wouldn't mind, say "ashes"?

MOXLEY: That isn't all that's left, so it was felt that
another expression...because there are bits of bone that
don't break down—
sometimes chunks...

DUNN: *(Imagining the campaign)*
Ashes and Chunks—the Suicidal Person's breakfast
cereal...

MOXLEY: I'm sorry, I didn't hear you...?

DUNN: *(Covering over)*
And the chunks of my "friend" would be where?—
if you don't have them?

MOXLEY: We have to dispose of them.
We have limited storage capacity—

DUNN: You dispose of them? Meaning, you scatter
them?
Or you haul them off to the local dump—

MOXLEY: If you wanted them, Mister Dunn—
why did you wait
for more than a year?

*(MS FISHER enters, carrying a small rectangular gray plastic
box. MOXLEY's relieved.)*

MOXLEY: You found them?

MS FISHER: *(Eyeing DUNN)*
You don't wanta know where.
They don't pay me enough.

I'm serious.
Let's just say—that "urban myth" about
alligators down there? Not a myth.

(We go back:)

MOXLEY: You found them?

MS FISHER: Lucky for somebody, they were mislabeled.
So they hadn't been pulled.

DUNN: But wait—if the label is wrong—

MOXLEY: *(Anticipating the question)*
Not the name—the date of disposal.
This *is* your friend.

DUNN: Smaller than I remember him.
More rectangular.
And—well, I mean, back then—
I said I wanted this? Cheap plastic?

MOXLEY: You said you weren't going to put him on
your mantle...

DUNN: No, probably not.
(Pause)
Did I happen, at the time, to mention what I was gonna
do with him?

MS FISHER: You said you were going to take him down
to the beach,
where you met, that summer...
(Pointing to her boss:)
Lurch pointed out that wouldn't be legal.
"O K, so you'd wait until sundown."
Though you wondered, if a wind came up—
it might blow him back, in your eyes, in your hair, in
your mouth,
you might even be breathing him in.
That's when Lurch brought out the Star Of The Ocean
Dissolvable Urn.

MOXLEY: You don't have to touch the ashes at all,
you just chuck the whole thing in.

MS FISHER: You told us to fuck ourselves.
So we sold you a low-end model, instead.

DUNN: Like a skull: put it there on my desk—
"Remember that you must write..."
David couldn't *stop* writing—
he was a gusher. I was a dripper...
(Of the urn)
This—thing is so ugly, why does it look like a paper
shredder?

(We go back:)

MS FISHER: You said you were going to take him down
to the beach,
where you met, that summer...

DUNN: No. I already lost him once—

MOXLEY: *Misplaced* him...

DUNN: —which is worse!

MS FISHER: That's true.

DUNN: I want him near to hand.
Forget the beach.

(The lights change.)

Scene Nine

(TATE's apartment
He sits in the chair, holding the portable phone.
He looks like he hasn't slept.
He stares at the phone, willing it to ring. It doesn't.
Finally he stands, puts the phone down on the chair, starts to
exit.
The phone rings.

TATE *stops, refusing to look at it. It keeps ringing.*
Reluctant, TATE *returns to the chair.*
He picks up the phone, opens the back, rips the batteries out.
The phone stops ringing.
TATE *tries to relax.*
Then a cell-phone in his pocket starts to ring: Fur Elise.
TATE *freezes.*
Finally, he takes the cell-phone out of his pocket, stares at it.
The phone keeps ringing.
The lights change.)

Scene Ten

*(*DUNN's *apartment.* DUNN *sits in a chair, holding the*
box-like urn in his lap.
He hesitates—then unlatches the box, opens the lid, looks in.)

DUNN: They put the cremains in a baggie?
(Gingerly, he pulls out the top of a large plastic bag.)
Not even a zip-lock? A twistie-thing?
Are they—they have got to be—...
(He undoes the twistie, opens the bag.
Then, gritting his teeth, he touches the ashes with his
fingertips.)
No, I guess they aren't.
They said there were chunks. There are...
God. So I wonder: that piece of bone—

(A loud knock at the door.)

TATE: *(Offstage)* Mister Dunn? I think you were
pounding on my wall, last night. Could I talk to you?

(Flustered, DUNN *puts the urn on the floor, goes to the door*
and opens it. TATE's *standing there, a paper bag in one hand.)*

TATE: Hey. I'm the neighbor from hell. Name is Tate.

(He offers his hand. DUNN, *seeing the ash on his own hand,*
doesn't take it.)

DUNN: *(Awkward)* Oh...

TATE: But apparently you know who I am.

DUNN: I don't.

TATE: You wouldn't shake my hand.

(DUNN shows his ash-covered hand.)

DUNN: I'm sorry. Dust. I was—cleaning house, Mister—
Tate. Should I know you?

TATE: Maybe I'm paranoid.
But people stare at me, on the subway.
(He decides to close the subject.)
Forget it. I just wanted to apologize—for the racket.

DUNN: You like heavy metal?

TATE: No. I like to—not think, for awhile. You know
what I mean?

DUNN: I do. I have a large mallet for that. I bonk myself
on the head...

TATE: Your apartment—was empty at first, when I
moved in.
I got used to that.
Not having to be considerate, I mean.

DUNN: Understood. It's O K.

TATE: *(Handing DUNN the paper bag)*
Anyway—peace offering?
Just a bottle of wine.

DUNN: A loaf of bread, and thou—
my *god*, you're a handsome man—
in the wilderness...

(We go back:)

TATE: Just a bottle of wine.

DUNN: I don't drink.

TATE: Oh.

DUNN: *(Quickly, to cover his gaffe)*
But thank you! I'll keep it for company.
Maybe some night, if you want to stop by...

TATE: *(Nodding)*
O K, well I'll let you get back to—whatever.
Were you unpacking?

DUNN: No—I'm a writer. Lap-top, months's supply of
Cheetos, case of Red Bull—this is it.

(Pause)

TATE: Word of advice—don't keep the remains.

DUNN: Excuse me?

TATE: That's an urn?

(DUNN nods.)

TATE: So—you've survived whoever that is.
Tough luck. Your life goes on.

DUNN: *(Disagreeing)*
Just now, I felt a—piece of bone...
Pelvis.
Maybe...
And can I get from there, back to—
it was hot, it was summer, it was his hipbone grinding
into me, that very first night, when he made me
understand
I'd never die?
I don't think so. I don't think there's a way—
to go back...

(We go back:)

TATE: Tough luck. Your life goes on.

(DUNN is startled—something has jogged his memory.)

DUNN: I *do* know you. Don't I?
That's why your name... My mind doesn't work
anymore:
"THROAT-SLITTING 101—COLLEGE PROF
IS NUMBER ONE SUSPECT."

TATE: You read the *Post.*

DUNN: For the poetry: "Headless Body In Topless Bar..."

(Pause)

TATE: Not that it matters, but just so you don't have to
triple-lock your door:
I'm innocent, Mister Dunn.

DUNN: Must be nice. I wish I could say the same.

(TATE lets himself out. DUNN sits down again.)

DUNN: Dear Diary: exciting news!
I live next door to a psychopath.
*(He imagines typing words on a screen, speaking the words
as he types:)*
Fade in:
Exterior. Deserted street. An autumn night.
Andrea, an attractive young student, walks down an
empty urban street, chatting on her cell-phone... *(Pause)*
And Andrea says...what does Andrea say?

(As DUNN wonders, the lights change.)

Scene Eleven

*(A subway car. DUNN approaches SELMA, who's been trying
not to meet his eye.)*

SELMA: Now you're stalking me?

DUNN: You won't take my calls.

SELMA: Uh-huh. And that would be telling you what?

DUNN: *(A neutral subject)*
You ride the subway...

SELMA: All my life. I have to stay in touch with the little people. So I can pander to them.

DUNN: I'm working on something new.

SELMA: A feel-good comedy about AIDS.

DUNN: You like mysteries, right?

SELMA: About?

DUNN: Ivy League scandal—sexy older guy—

SELMA: Harrison Ford?

DUNN: Not *that* old—
—who may or may not have butchered a student.

SELMA: O K, right outa the gate, the "may or may not" would be a problem. People don't like ambiguity.

DUNN: I'll resolve it. Though in real life—

SELMA: *(As it dawns)*
Back up—is this a true story?

DUNN: "Ripped from the headlines"

SELMA: Marcus Tate?

DUNN: Ta-da!

SELMA: I had a run-in with that guy:
dead eyes like a shark. He threatened to kill me.

DUNN: But he didn't. Professional courtesy?

SELMA: I already packaged that story, for a cheesy Lifetime movie. James Brolin, playing Harrison Ford, And—O K, she's a little long in the tooth for the co-ed—what's-her-fang—Buffy...

DUNN: Who's writing it?

SELMA: Nobody you know.
Somebody with a career.

DUNN: They have access to Marcus Tate?

SELMA: No. He won't talk.

(DUNN *grins.*)

SELMA: In your wet dreams, you mean.

DUNN: In the attractive flesh.

SELMA: So—you're drinking again. That's sad.

DUNN: No.

SELMA: *The* Marcus Tate.

DUNN: With the dead shark eyes.

(*A homelss man—looking unsteady—enters the car and surveys the terrain.*)

SELMA: I'm guessing, in your version, the student's a guy?

DUNN: Surprise! A woman.

SELMA: He had sex with her...

DUNN: I'm not sure, yet.

SELMA: No, I'm saying—he had sex with her.
Knock out a draft, we'll talk in a couple of weeks.
One thing: this whacko—
he's O K with you writing about him?

DUNN: Well...

SELMA: Beautiful. So—when he finds out?

HOMELESS MAN: Ladies and gentlemen? If I could kindly have your attention? Thank you.
I don't wanta hurt anyone...

SELMA: Always good news...

DUNN: It's O K—he's a friend of mine.

(The lights change.)

Scene Twelve

(The hallway of DUNN's *apartment.)*

*(*DUNN *approaches his door, when he hears a tremendous crash from* TATE's *apartment.)*

*(*DUNN *shakes his head, unlocks his door. Just then, another loud crash from* TATE's *apartment.)*

*(*DUNN *crosses to* TATE's *door, gives a tentative knock.)*

DUNN: Mister Tate? Are you all right?

*(*DUNN *stands in the hallway, uncertain, as* TATE *doesn't answer.)*

(The elderly MRS ROTH *opens her door a crack, looks out.)*

MRS ROTH: U P S?

DUNN: No, Mrs Roth—it's your neighbor—
Edward Dunn—

MRS ROTH: Then with the racket, already—stop!

(She shuts the door in DUNN's *face. We hear her now, through the door:)*

MRS ROTH: Simba! Put the mouse *down.*

(Shrugging, DUNN *starts to go back to his place, when* TATE *comes out of his room and into the hall.)*

TATE: You want something?

DUNN: No—I just heard a crash. Or two.
I wondered if you were O K.

TATE: Hey, you should see the other guy.
(Pause)
I wish there was another guy.
Somebody I could challenge, someone I could fight...

fuckit. *FUCK.*
(In his frustration, he bangs the wall.)

MRS ROTH: *(Off)* U P S?

DUNN: No!
(Seizing the moment—to TATE:*)*
You wanta come in? Kick over a chair?
Have a glass of wine?

TATE: I don't drink alone. And you don't indulge.

DUNN: I also have tap-water.
Best in the world, they say: New York tap...

TATE: ...which gives you pause...

DUNN: Is that a no?

(As DUNN *waits for* TATE's *answer,* MRS ROTH—
ever hopeful—opens her door a crack.)

MRS ROTH: U P S?

(The lights change.)

Scene Thirteen

*(*DUNN's *apartment.* DUNN's *offstage, getting drinks.)*

*(*TATE *sits in the only chair, looking around.)*

*(*DUNN—*trying for casual—speaks from offstage:)*

DUNN: *(Off, a question)*
So—things've been hard.

TATE: "What doesn't kill us, fucks us up so bad,
we wish we were brave enough to kill ourselves,
but we're not."

DUNN: *(Off)* That's Nietzsche, right?

*(*TATE *laughs, as* DUNN *re-enters with glasses of water.)*

TATE: Things've been tough. Yeah, I guess:
no wife anymore, no job, no possibility of another job—
not until I've been cleared, but I can't be cleared,
because I've never been charged.

DUNN: I still don't understand why you're a suspect.

(Pause)

TATE: "Because I was there."
In her life, I mean—a small part of it—
and they think she knew the killer.

DUNN: But didn't she have family—friends?
They knew her...

TATE: I do bring that up.
But Americans like to believe their teachers are evil.
I gotta take a leak.

DUNN: "Evil?"

TATE: *(As he's moving off)*
And their own children are worse.
Without the slightest capacity to choose between right
and wrong.
(He's exited, now speaking from offstage.)
Blank slates—except for the acne—
on which we get to scrawl our wicked thoughts.

(TATE is gone. DUNN wonders if he's getting any closer.)

DUNN: *(Calling out:)* Like what?

TATE: *(Off)* Sorry?

(The off-stage toilet flushes. DUNN considers, then yells:)

DUNN: What wicked thoughts?

*(No answer. ANDREA, twenty, enters—on her
cell-phone—passing DUNN, who watches, mesmerized.
ANDREA waits for an overdue bus, talking into her phone.)*

ANDREA: No, I got away with it!
He was afraid. And that's all I wanted.
(...)
I could tell, because—wait, I think my bus...
(She looks out.)
No. And I'm freezing my ass off.
(...)
I dunno, a half-hour, fuckit, I'm walking.
(She heads off down the dark street.)
Anyway—it was his hands. They were shaking. Bad.
That's how I knew.
They'd do that in "the Gulf", he was always telling us,
when he swam up to a mine.
(...)
In the Gulf. Of Persia.
(...)
Oh, you mean where am *I*?
(She glances around.)
Passing that old cemetery—
(...)
No, there are people around—
(Seeing that there aren't)
—or there were: ok, do you want me to freak?
(...)
Because I always walk home this way—
and the sad thing is? The dead stay dead.
Kurt Cobain will never hold me in his skanky arms.
(Walking a little faster)
And now I'm rounding Papaya King—
(...)
—yes, I'm already through the "bad" neighborhood,
if—I'm assuming by "bad", you mean black?
(...)
Fine. You're not a racist—you're a realist.
That's what a racist always says.
(...)
No, I'm pretty sure I was always a bitch.

You were slow to pick up on it.
(...)
Bigoted and stupid—right.
It's possible I hate everyone.
(...)
The last fucking leaves are falling—how's that?
And I try to tell the truth—
because it's important—
and nobody cares!
(...)
You do not! The "bad" neighborhood?
What is that?
Or "the Gulf?" "When I was in the Gulf—"
And I'm like, "Professor Tate,
I don't want to hear war-stories—
I want you to tell me what I'm *doing* here!—
on this planet, at this screwed-up moment in time—
And I know you've been lying to us—"

*(Suddenly a man in a ski mask [*TATE*] runs up to* ANDREA.
*He grabs her from behind, holding an [unseen] knife to her
throat.*
ANDREA *freezes, terrified.* DUNN *watches, also afraid.)*

TATE: Slash her throat *this* way—
(Miming the action)
—and tonight it's cold enough,
that the hot—that the, blood—
it comes out smoking...
fountaining up and out and into the dark...

(He releases his hold on ANDREA, *she doesn't move.*
TATE *stares at her. Then, pulling off his mask, he turns to*
DUNN.)*

TATE: So that's one version...
That's the one Detective Munoz likes the best.

DUNN: But there's no evidence, is there?
What you just said—it's all speculation...

TATE: Not all of it.
They found the girl she was talking to, on the phone.

DUNN: And the victim said those things?
She wanted to make you afraid... why?

(TATE *says nothing.*)

DUNN: What did you do to her?

TATE: Nothing.

DUNN: She said, "You've been lying to us—" About
what?

(ANDREA *comes out of her trance, looks at* TATE.)

ANDREA: *(Into phone)*
I dunno, a half hour, fuckit, I'm walking.
(She heads off down the dark street.)
Anyway—it was his hands.
They were shaking. Bad. That's how I knew.
(She's gone.)

(DUNN *stares at* TATE.)

DUNN: You met with her that afternoon...
And she confronted you—about what?

(Pause)

TATE: She was disappointed in me.

DUNN: Because...

TATE: I was trying to teach her how to think—
by challenging her assumptions...
all her unexamined beliefs.
She said that left her with nothing.
And that made me just as bad as her parents.
Out of touch, conservative—
she even accused me of being a hawk.
I told her that I might've been—
but that was before a friend of mine—
my swimming buddy, from training school—

had a leg blown off, in the first Gulf War.
He bled to death right in front of me,
and all I could do was hold his hand—
and I'm screaming, "Fuck! Oh fuck..."

DUNN: I'm sorry.

TATE: Would that the government were—
we're still waiting for an apology.
Given the fact that our boat-crew was hit by "friendly
fire."

(DUNN *doesn't know what to say.*)

TATE: As the young'uns say—shit happens.
But I guess you know all about it, huh?
(*He starts to move off.*)
I'll take a rain-check on the tap-water.

DUNN: Why?

TATE: I talk too much.

DUNN: But—doesn't it help?

TATE: You mean, does the rocket hang in the air?
Does my buddy see it hanging,
still have time to walk out from under it,
back to his wife and his two little girls
and live out the rest of his boring, happy life—
if I talk about it?
(*Pause*)
You're a writer...

DUNN: Yes—

TATE: Are you trying to write about me?
Because—if you are—fuck you.

(DUNN *can't answer.* TATE *exits.*
A moment—then DUNN *shouts after him.*)

DUNN: The rocket falls! Your buddy blows up!
Tough luck! Your life goes on!
(He falls silent, wishing he hadn't blown it.)

(The lights change.)

Scene Fourteen

(TATE and DUNN, in their separate beds, with the [unseen] wall between them.)

(TATE is punching numbers into his portable phone. DUNN's bedside phone starts ringing.)

DUNN: *(Answering, foggy)*
Hello?

TATE: So tell me about your lover.

(DUNN, startled, takes a second to focus. But then he plays along, hoping to re-establish contact.)

DUNN: I never had one.

TATE: The guy in the urn?

DUNN: How do you know I'm gay?
Am I wearing a sign on my back?

TATE: Yeah, you are—two signs:
one says, "Gay"...

DUNN: And the other?

TATE: "Kick me."

DUNN: —which you're glad to do.

TATE: So you loved him? You hated him? You put up with
him? All the above?

DUNN: I killed him.
He was a smoker. He was a drinker.
I let him continue.

TATE: You were funneling the booze down his throat?
Shoving a lit cigarette in his mouth?

DUNN: He badgered people. Like you do.

TATE: Answer the question!

DUNN: Fine! He killed *himself!*

TATE: Bingo! But, then you ask yourself why:
why, dear God, did he have to check out?
And what does God whisper to you,
when you're lying awake, late at night,
in your empty bed?
(Putting his hand to his ear)
—I'm sorry, God—say again?—
"BECAUSE HE DIDN'T LOVE YOU ENOUGH!"
(Pause)
How did he die?

DUNN: You don't know me.

TATE: Down to the ground.
He died of what?

(Pause)

DUNN: Lung cancer. Not a good way to go.
Diagnosed in April—dead in December:
gone, goodbye.
In terrible pain the whole time,
and it kept getting worse—
so did his breathing—
the doctor said, at the end, he was drowning—
twisted up in his bed-sheets flopping around
like a fish about to be clubbed...

(Pause)

TATE: "Kick me."

DUNN: Go to hell.

TATE: No—dwell on how he died.
Forget about how he lived.

DUNN: He wouldn't let me get away with anything.
No bullshit.
It's hard to live without bullshit.
How do you do it, Mister Tate?

(He hangs up, shaken.
After a moment, he gets out of bed—determined—and starts
to get dressed.
In his bedroom, TATE stares up at the dark. Then he dials
DUNN's number again.
DUNN ignores the phone, continues dressing. The lights
change.)

Scene Fifteen

(A gay bar. DUNN looks around, uncomfortable. A HUSTLER
approaches him.)

HUSTLER: How's it goin'?

DUNN: "Come here often?" "What's your sign?"

HUSTLER: Whatever. Fuck you.
(He starts to move off.)

DUNN: Wait—I'm sorry—

HUSTLER: Forget it. I wasn't hitting on you.
You're too old.

(Pause)

DUNN: O K. It's just—I'm not—
I haven't—done this. For a long time.

HUSTLER: You need a coupla pointers?

(DUNN nods.)

HUSTLER: Well, if you didn't come off like an angry shithead, from the word "go", that'd help.

(Pause)

DUNN: You're very beautiful.

HUSTLER: No, I'm not. I'm just young.
And you're horny as fuck.

(Pause)

DUNN: Can you help me?

(The HUSTLER *gives him a card.)*

HUSTLER: I do Swedish massage.

DUNN: With "full release"?

HUSTLER: That's an extra fifty.

*(*DUNN *pulls out his wallet.)*

HUSTLER: You don't pay me now.

DUNN: *(Offering cash)*
Take it. Please.
Before I chicken out.

(Reluctantly, the HUSTLER *takes the cash.)*

DUNN: Thanks. I'm a cop. And you're under arrest.

(The HUSTLER *fights a moment of panic.)*

HUSTLER: You're full of it. Show me a badge.

DUNN: I don't need no stinkin' badges.

(Pause)

HUSTLER: Yeah, O K. This is funny to you?

DUNN: I get tired of being the only one who's looking over his shoulder.

HUSTLER: What've you done?

DUNN: I lived too long.

HUSTLER: So here's my question, man:
you don't wanta get laid.
What do you want?

(Pause)

DUNN: This guy I used to—know—
I'd fall asleep in his arms, every night,
or he'd drift off in mine...

HUSTLER: Like—how do you mean—like this?

(The HUSTLER *stands behind* DUNN, *wraps his arms around him, resting his head on* DUNN's *shoulder.)*

HUSTLER: And what would he say?
Tell me.

(Pause. DUNN—*almost painfully—is relaxing into the* HUSTLER's *arms.)*

DUNN: "When it was over"—dot, dot, dot—
he'd say, "I wanta spoon you."
I'd let him curl around me...
feel his breath on my neck,
and the beat of his heart—
he was out of shape, so his heart would pound—
and even that was a comfort...
the heat of him, and the smell of his skin...
and we did that, how many nights,
for how many years, and then it was gone...
And I thought— "Why not? Pick up a whore,
maybe get infected—join him..."

(We go back:)

HUSTLER: And what would he say?
Tell me.
"I'm going to die and leave you alone, you old and
angry shithead.
Everybody's going to leave you behind.
Sooner or later."

(We go back:)

HUSTLER: Tell me.

DUNN: He'd say, "So—you've survived... Tough luck.
Your life goes on..."
(Pause)
No—wait! That was somebody else...
(He pulls away, unsettled.)

HUSTLER: You already got a somebody else?

DUNN: No!

HUSTLER: You stud.
So life goes on.

DUNN: No, it doesn't. It can't.
(Pause)
He's straight. And also a psychopath.

HUSTLER: The good ones always are.

*(The HUSTLER pulls DUNN back into an embrace. But now
DUNN can't relax.
The lights change.)*

Scene Sixteen

*(DUNN's apartment
DUNN has returned from his strike-out at the bar.
He holds a portable phone in his hand. Finishing up a debate
[in his head], he punches in a number.
The phone in TATE's bedroom rings.
Groggy, TATE wakes up, grabs for his phone.)*

TATE: Hello?

*(DUNN—suddenly feeling unsure of himself—doesn't
answer.)*

TATE: Oh. It's you.
How's it going in hell? Hot?

Or did Dante nail it—is it frozen, at the core?
(Pause)
I know, after what you did to me,
you didn't go to Heaven.

(DUNN *listens in, fascinated.*)

TATE: I never told anybody this,
but I'm glad you're dead. Delirious.
If I knew where you were buried,
I'd do a two-step on your grave.
Lob a few grenades—why not?
Commando from the Black Lagoon—
in my wet-suit and my flippers...
(Pause) What did you think would happen to me,
if you told the world?
Did you care?
(Pause)
Of course, it's happening anyway.
You stopped me dead in my tracks.
(Pause)
People go on for awhile, though,
after they stop. That's a problem.
How to fill the hours, till the cops decide to arrest me?
Wipe off the random fingerprint or two,
get rid of the evidence—
what the cops would *think* was evidence,
given their already-low opinion...

(DUNN, *listening in, is more and more alarmed.*)

TATE: I'd say, "Pleasant dreams"—but I hope what you
see
is one hand suddenly clamping your mouth,
and the other holding the knife,
very close to your throat—

(DUNN *is so unnerved, he clicks off the phone.*)

TATE: Hello?

(DUNN *stands there, holding the turned-off phone.*
TATE *thinks for a moment—then he punches in "Star-6-9".*
DUNN's *phone begins to ring.* DUNN *jumps, dropping the*
phone.
It keeps ringing. He picks it up like a bomb about to go off.
It keeps ringing. He finally clicks it "on", but doesn't speak.)

TATE: Dunn? Is that you?

(DUNN *doesn't answer.)*

TATE: I'm not angry...I understand:
only so many hours one can spend
watching Lifetime movies—
dusting your partner's urn—
you run out of things to do.
So you pick up the phone, and you call someone—
in the wee small hours, night after night—

DUNN: I've never—done this before—

TATE: You're doing it now.
Phone rings, my heart starts pounding,
nobody's there. But you.

(Pause)

DUNN: You said you got rid of—evidence—
something incriminating?...
What was it?

(Pause)

TATE: I had a K-bar. The cops are thinking
she may have been killed with a K-bar.
I panicked. So I took mine down to the river,
and I threw it in.
Stupid move, *n'est-ce pas*?

DUNN: Because...

TATE: Maybe that knife would have cleared me.
Forensics could've proved it wasn't the murder weapon.
Now it's gone.

(Pause)

DUNN: What was Andrea Evans going to "tell the world" about you?

(TATE *doesn't answer.*)

DUNN: You said you were glad she was dead.
"Delirious." I *heard* you.
(Silence)
She found out something... What?

TATE: I'd tell you, Mister Dunn—
but then I'd have to kill you.

DUNN: Seriously?

(No answer)

DUNN: Would you?

(Silence)

DUNN: You told me she was "disappointed" in you.

(TATE *says nothing.*)

DUNN: But it was more than that.
She was threatening you.
So maybe you *did* have a motive, after all.
(Pause)
She sees the blade of the knife—
just for a second—
and in the reflection:
someone is standing behind her...
why am I seeing *you*?

(Pause)

TATE: Call the cops. Tell them what you heard.
You fucking—writer.
And if they wanta pick me up,
I'll be at that elegant whorehouse
they all know about, on East Fifty-Eighth.
(He clicks off the phone in disgust, throws it down.

Then, half-dressed, he grabs some clothes and hurries out of the room.
A moment later, DUNN *can hear* TATE'*s door, as it opens and closes.*
DUNN *stands in the dark, not knowing what to do.*
The lights change.)

Scene Seventeen

(A hooker's hotel room.)

*(*TATE *has just had sex with a* HOOKER. *He's getting dressed—she watches him.)*

HOOKER: I think you left marks.

TATE: Sorry.

HOOKER: So what's your problem.

TATE: Could we not talk?

HOOKER: You didn't pay for not talking.

TATE: How much would that be?

HOOKER: A lot more than you got.
(Pause)
I know who you are.

TATE: I thought maybe you did.

HOOKER: I fucked Bernard Goetz.

TATE: Dating yourself.

HOOKER: He was better than you.
And he was bad.

TATE: Who else?

HOOKER: Well—Klaus von Bulow.
But everybody did him.
So I don't take much credit for that.

TATE: Anyone in the last decade?

HOOKER: *(Shrugs)*
Kobe Bryant. But way before...
I useta be better-lookin'.

(TATE looks out an [unseen] window.)

TATE: You have enemies?

HOOKER: Who doesn't?

TATE: Somebody's out there—watching your window.

HOOKER: Maybe it's you they want—like, one of the
relatives, of the girl you killed.

TATE: "Allegedly" killed.

HOOKER: Yeah—like that.

TATE: Right. Did I make you cum?

HOOKER: Oh honey...

TATE: *(Imitating her)*
"Yes! Yes! Yes! Yes!"

HOOKER: *(Imitating him)*
"Allegedly! Allegedly!"

(Pause)

TATE: You knew who I was.
And they never found the murder weapon.
Maybe I have it.
(He makes the slashing motion with his hand.)

HOOKER: So what? It'd be a vacation.
I wake up in the morning, I think,
"Oh fuck—again?"

TATE: *(Agreeing)*
Open my eyes: "I'm still here?"
(Pause)
Did anyone ever love you?

HOOKER: Oh honey...

(TATE *glances out the window again.*)

TATE: I know that guy.

HOOKER: What guy?

TATE: On the sidewalk. Looking up at the window.

HOOKER: *You* have a stalker? Isn't that backwards?

TATE: He's a writer.

HOOKER: Oh. Sorry.

TATE: He didn't call the cops—I wonder why.

HOOKER: Did you confess?

(*Pause*)

(TATE *leans out the window.* DUNN *appears below, looking up.*)

TATE: Hey you! Taking notes down there—
why didn't you call the cops, when you had a chance?
This hooker's lying here in a pool of blood, the flies are
buzzing...

HOOKER: I think—all things considered—
you should get the fuck out. O K?

(*Ignoring her,* TATE *climbs into the window, seemingly ready to jump.*)

TATE: (*Still calling down to* DUNN)
And now, before I hear the SWAT team thundering up
the stairs...

HOOKER: Perfect end to a perfect day.
(*Exiting:*)
Hey Bruno! We got a jumper!

(*She's gone.* TATE *looks down, his dark joke getting more serious.*)

TATE: Yeah, maybe we do...
Every morning, open my eyes:
why am I still here?
(He leans further out, his perch even more precarious.)
In this body, on this planet—
(Remembering)
—what did she say:
"At this fucked-up moment in time..."

(DUNN calls up:)

DUNN: I stand away, as far as I can,
from the edge of the subway platform...
I don't go near an open window—
because—it would be too easy:
take one step in front of the train, out the window,
gone, good-bye...

TATE: Isn't that what you want?

DUNN: But I'm a coward, Mister Tate! Are you?
(Pause)
Weren't you trained as a diver?

TATE: So what?

DUNN: So—if you're innocent—
don't *you* want to find the knife?

*(TATE teeters on the sill, startled at first—and then amazed
that DUNN is caught up.
The lights change.)*

Scene Eighteen

*(A rowboat, on the Hudson. Night
DUNN, wary, sits in the boat, steadying it with an oar. TATE
surfaces, in minimal diving gear [trunks and face-mask],
holds on to the side of the boat.)*

DUNN: Can you see anything?

TATE: Not much. Maybe the current moved it further down.

DUNN: Shine your light in my face.

TATE: Why?

DUNN: I want to know if I'm afraid.

TATE: You can't tell?

DUNN: Not anymore. No.

(TATE *shines his portable floodlight on* DUNN'*s face.*
DUNN'*s expression is hard to read.*)

TATE: You look like you're waiting for something.

DUNN: The world to end.

TATE: Or the world to begin...

DUNN: *(Reminding)* Knife?

(TATE *goes under again.* DUNN *watches him disappear.*
Behind DUNN, *a tarpaulin moves, on the bottom of the boat.*
ANDREA *crawls out.* DUNN *doesn't look at her, but he*
knows she's there. ANDREA *lights up a cigarette.*)

ANDREA: You can smoke in hell. In fact, it's required.
One of the advantages.

(DUNN *tries to get rid of her.*)

DUNN: Name one of the people Jeffrey Dahmer ate.
Beep—time's up.
Or one of Ted Bundy's co-eds:
pick a body. Any body.
(Pause)
The killers live forever.
And the victims fade away.
I know you suffered and died.
And that's all I know.
Get out of the boat.
(Pause)

ANDREA: I've spent some time with your friend—David.
He's funny.

DUNN: David's in hell?

ANDREA: And sexy, in that kind of mournful Irish
way—
with that lantern jaw...

(Pause)

DUNN: We went to Ireland, once—it was a pilgrimage,
he was in love with Yeats.
I have a curled-up Polaroid of him dancing on Yeats'
grave...

ANDREA: Yeats is funny, too.
Again, with that gloomy Celtic thing going on—

DUNN: David's in hell? With Yeats?

ANDREA: And everyone else I ever knew.

(Pause)

DUNN: Shine a light in my face—oh god—
see, this is what I was afraid of...
After my mother died, my father went quietly insane...
Closed up most of the house—
and he lived in a single room, like a squatter...
Writing her all these letters I found—
asking her when she was coming back.

ANDREA: He died?

DUNN: A year after she did. Heart attack.

ANDREA: And now you think you're due?

(Pause)

DUNN: Why have you come back?
Are you here to tell me—
did he kill you?

(ANDREA *is silent.*)

DUNN: Why won't David come back?
Why can't I see him, when I close my eyes?

ANDREA: Maybe he hasn't forgiven you.

DUNN: *(Stricken)*
For what? *(Pause)* For *what*?

(Suddenly TATE *explodes up out of the water, grabbing*
ANDREA, *slashing her throat.*
This time the wound is real—blood sprays everywhere.
ANDREA *staggers against the side of the boat,* TATE *pulls her*
into the water. Both of them disappear.
DUNN *doesn't move. He's in shock.*
Long pause
TATE *resurfaces.*
We go back:)

DUNN: Shine your light in my face.

TATE: Why?

DUNN: I want to know if I'm afraid.

TATE: You can't tell?

DUNN: Not anymore.

*(*TATE *shines his portable floodlight on* DUNN's *face.*
DUNN's *expression is hard to read.)*

TATE: You look like you're waiting for something.

DUNN: The world to end.

TATE: Or the world to begin...

DUNN: Knife?

*(*TATE *goes under again.* DUNN *watches him disappear.*
Water-sounds—splashing, the creak of a pier, gulls...
ANDREA *doesn't come back.*
DUNN *waits, more and more anxious.*
Finally TATE *resurfaces, deeply discouraged.)*

TATE: Nothing. Tires, shopping carts...
Jimmy Hoffa in a block of cement...

DUNN: Then it's gone.
Nobody will find it.

(Pause)

TATE: I didn't kill her. I swear.
But sometimes—late at night—
when the phone is ringing—
I think I did.
(Pause)
Help me. Please.

DUNN: How?

TATE: I need an alibi...
Don't you?

(The lights change.)

Scene Nineteen

(An interrogation room
The DETECTIVE *is questioning* DUNN.*)*

DETECTIVE: ...You move in, you meet the guy next door,
you like him—I'm doin' O K, so far?

*(*DUNN *nods.)*

DETECTIVE: Even though you realize he's a suspect in a
murder case.
And you realize, because—
you keep seeing his picture, in the *Post.*

DUNN: Yes, but if what you're implying is—

DETECTIVE: Whoa! Bear with me, O K? Because I'm not
a writer,
I'm just a dumb cop...but I'm wondering why—at this
late date—

you suddenly have this memory of meeting the suspect
earlier:
this total stranger, one night in a bar—
and the night and the hour just happen to be the time
when Andrea Evans was killed.
And you remember the man, and the night and the hour
even though he only said three words to you,
and you said four?
 "Got a light?"
"Sorry, I don't smoke."
Burned into your brain.

(Pause)

DUNN: It was the first anniversary...

DETECTIVE: Of?

DUNN: The day my partner died.

DETECTIVE: And you're out celebrating...

DUNN: I fell off the wagon. I got drunk.
Fuck you.

(Pause)

DETECTIVE: O K—you remember the day for a reason.
Why remember the guy?

(Pause)

DUNN: I was startled—when he sat down.

DETECTIVE: Because...

DUNN: He reminded me, of...David.
Not physicaly...
something about the way he held himself—
the way he smiled...
telling the bartender lousy jokes—
he seemed to be very—glad, to be in the world.
David was like that, once...
"Kangaroo walks into a bar—"

DETECTIVE: A year ago... And it took that long to
fabricate this totally bullshit alibi?
(Pause)
You go down on him?

DUNN: Yes.

DETECTIVE: *(Taken aback)*
I don't think so.

DUNN: Salt, and sweat, and that coppery
onion-funk of a man, and big —
not that that matters, of course, but—big—
imposing—and it had been a long time.
I'd been wondering, if I would
ever get back to that place—
where I was alive...

(We go back:)

DETECTIVE: You go down on him?
Why do you wanta protect him?
The guy is a menace. Swear to god.
And giving false evidence happens to be a crime.
Were you aware of that?

DUNN: You still haven't found the murder weapon,
right?
And you have no motive.
And no evidence. You can't arrest him.
All you can do is harass him:
till he's stripped of friends, and family,
and a job, and even a future...

DETECTIVE: Why were you out on the river, last night?

(DUNN reacts.)

DETECTIVE: You don't think we're watching you?

DUNN: Did you see—was there a—woman, in the boat?

(The DETECTIVE looks at him like he's crazy.)

DUNN: Never mind.

DETECTIVE: You rely on your gut, as a writer?
I gotta rely on my mine.
And the very first time I met the guy,
I knew. He was the one.
So—you wanta give it another shot?
Tell me the truth?

(DUNN *takes a deep breath, decides to stay with his story.*)

DUNN: Man walks into a bar.
Good-looking man, but he's straight,
and I'm still in mourning.
Says, "Got a light?"
I say, "I don't smoke."
Though I'm thinking, long as I'm falling off the wagon,
maybe I'll start again...
I look up at the clock—and here's where it
starts to get strange—it's 10:17.
Exactly when—a year ago—I was putting on my coat,
to go home for the night,
and then I looked over at David—
and he was gone. While my back was turned.
In the time it took me to button up an overcoat.
Just a body.

DETECTIVE: So Marcus Tate was with you, from 10:17—

DUNN: Till we closed the bar. One o'clock.

DETECTIVE: "Got a light?" "I don't smoke".
That was it, for three hours?

(DUNN *nods.*)

DETECTIVE: And you won't change your story?

DUNN: No.

(*Pause*)

DETECTIVE: O K, and I'm just asking, but—
how are you gonna feel, when he kills again?

(The lights change.)

Scene Twenty

(DUNN's apartment. TATE has broken in. He's standing, reading DUNN's screenplay.
Behind him, ANDREA sits in a chair—as we first saw her, before she was killed—smoking a cigarette.
At the sound of a key turning in a lock, TATE looks up. But only a moment—then he goes back to his reading.
DUNN enters, takes in the scene. He's less surprised to see ANDREA than to see TATE.)

DUNN: *(To TATE)*
What are you doing?

TATE: Reading your screenplay.

(Pause)

DUNN: *(Unable to help himself)*
And...?
(Stopping himself)
Forget it!
You broke into my *apartment*?

TATE: With a credit-card. Get a dead-bolt.
Or maybe you aren't afraid of ghosts.

DUNN: *(Glancing at ANDREA)*
A door won't keep them out.

(TATE finally looks up.)

TATE: How does it end?

DUNN: I don't know. I keep coming back to that final phone-call. Where the victim was sad.
And she couldn't say why:
because the leaves were falling.
Or maybe because you had lied to her. About what?
(Pause)

ABOUT WHAT?
(Pause) I just got back from the precinct house.
They knew we were out on the water.

TATE: You tell them why?
Did you turn me in?

DUNN: I told the police you were with me, the night of
the murder.

TATE: *(Covering his surprise)*
They believe you?

DUNN: No.
(Pause)
But I said I'd testify in court.
So—you have an alibi.

*(Touched in spite of himself, TATE decides to come clean at
last.)*

TATE: O K. Listen...

*(He starts to recall his final meeting with ANDREA, the night
of her death.)*

ANDREA: What was he like? Your swimming buddy—
the guy who got his leg blown off—
some godforsaken beach in Kuwait,
and you were shouting, "Fuck—oh fuck..."
I found that very moving. Truly.
Only, it never happened.
You were in the Navy—
but 3rd Class Petty Officer, was as far as you got.
You were never a Navy SEAL.
You were never in combat.
Nobody died in your arms.
I found a site on the Web, where they're outing
wannabes—like you.

(Pause)

TATE: Ms Evans, are you crying?

ANDREA: No. Hay fever.

TATE: Can I—do anything?

(Pause)

ANDREA: Why would you tell stories—
about a war you were never in?

TATE: I thought, at some point, I'd tell my class the
truth:
that they'd all been had.
And the shock would teach them a couple of things:
never trust authority,
and always question your sources.
But the moment came, to reveal myself, and went.
This was many years ago.
And I found I was starting to like
this other person I was becoming.

ANDREA: But people died in that war, and you
pretend you suffered beside them?

TATE: I'm sorry, but can we table this
discussion for a decade or two?
By then, you may understand the temptation
to edit your life. When you've had a life.
(Pause)
I did train to be a SEAL, and I hung in there, up until
"Hell Week."
But my knees were shot —
they were swollen up like melons.
I washed out.

ANDREA: And you can't accept that,
so—you reinvent yourself as a hero?
Like some frat-boy president landing a jet on the deck
of an aircraft carrier?

TATE: He was performing. So am I, when I teach.

ANDREA: You mean you're lying.

TATE: If that's what it takes, to grab my students'
attention—yes, I lie.

ANDREA: But I never wanted to hear war-stories.
I wanted you—anyone—please—
to tell me what I'm *doing* here!
—in this body, on this planet, at this totally fucked-up
moment in time—
but you've been lying to us—

TATE: About my past. Nothing else.

ANDREA: Who are you?

(Pause)

TATE: Is this a matter between you and me, Ms Evans?
Or will you spread the word?

ANDREA: Are we in the Gulf right now, Professor Tate?
Your hands are shaking.

TATE: *(Finishing up his story)*
The very last thing she said to me.
And then she walked out into the night.

(Turning to DUNN, *he pulls out a knife.)*

DUNN: *(Alarmed)*
I thought—you threw that away.

TATE: No.

DUNN: Then why did we—go out on the water...?

TATE: You wanted to get to know me better.
And—I think you did.
(Pause. He points to the urn.)
Let's take your friend, go for a drive.
Up the coast, till we find a beach...
Isn't that where you met?

(DUNN hesitates, paralyzed.)

(ANDREA *pulls out a cell-phone. Standing up, she starts to talk, as she exits, passing the men.*)

ANDREA: No, I got away with it!
He was afraid. And that's all I wanted.

(*The men watch her go.*)

TATE: She knew who I was.
Now there's only you.

(*The lights change.*)

Scene Twenty-one

(*A beach. Dusk*)

(DUNN—*holding the plastic urn—looks out at the water.*)

(TATE *still has the knife in his hand.*)

TATE: Where did you meet? Some place like this?

DUNN: It doesn't matter.

(TATE *gestures with the knife.*)

TATE: Tell me.

(*Pause*)

DUNN: Up the coast, an hour or so—an old farmhouse,
on a rise...
twenty-five years ago, at a writers' retreat.
It was summer—hot as hell...

TATE: Go on.

DUNN: It was so dark, that summer—
I'd be running to meet him
down this endless lawn, to the beach...
And I could only find him, in the dark,
by the glow of his cigarette.
(*Pause*)
He'd look up—and his smile...

I barely remember it—
so many years ago...

(Pause)

TATE: Open the lid.
Scatter his ashes.
Do it. *Now.*

DUNN: And then what?
(Very deliberately, he puts the urn down on the beach.)
You killed her.

TATE: Yes.

(TATE slowly wraps himself around DUNN, holding him like the HUSTLER did—but with the knife to DUNN's throat.)

TATE: I grabbed her from behind—
held the knife to her throat...

(DUNN is so afraid, he starts to relax in TATE's arms— like the fear was gone and a loved one were holding him.)

DUNN: How could you watch her die? Did you?
See the light in her eyes go out...
it's there and then it's gone...
and you realize you're standing
at the edge of an abyss...

(TATE releases DUNN. We go back:)

DUNN: You killed her.

TATE: I wanted to.
I was nothing. So I invented a life.
And she intended to take it.
(Pause)
I watched her walk away. I almost—went after her.
I stopped myself.
But sometimes, late at night—
didn't you want to kill your friend?

(Pause)

DUNN: Our family doctor told me,
maybe a month before the end—
"He won't have any more good days—
and so much for modern medicine.
If he were a family pet, in this much pain,
you'd put him to sleep.
But he's not—so he has to keep suffering..."
I couldn't get that out of my head:
"He won't have any more good days..."
You were given a certain number—
and when you had used them up—...
(Pause)
He stayed at home, for as long as I could
care for him, by myself...
And then finally, he was so far gone
he had to enter a hospice...
where the people seemed to be kind—
I think they were—but they had to get used to
watching patients stumble away...
(Pause)
One night David shat himself,
and the aides tried out a new piece of equipment:
a metal tub with a water-tight door
on the side that you could open—
so the patient didn't have to step over the edge
of the tub, he could just walk into it—
we carried David down the hall—
and stripped off his gown,
and helped him sit—not easily—on this
little metal shelf...
And then the nurses' aides fiddled with
all these levers and valves
they'd only ever used for a practice run—
till they finally turned a wheel
and a jet of freezing water hit David—
he screamed and tried to get away,
the water was rising around his feet—

he could barely speak, but he was
trying to shout: "Cold! Cold!"
(Pause)
They were struggling with the controls,
trying to find the hot water, and laughing—
at their own incompetence, probably—
I realized later, but then—
they were laughing—David was jerking his head
from side to side, his eyes were wide...
he looked like a frightened animal...
And I could've shouted,
"What the fuck are you people doing? STOP THIS!"
(Pause)
I could've pulled him out of the water...
dried him off and held him in my arms,
till he was warm...
But I didn't. I didn't.
I couldn't move. I couldn't do—
anything. I don't know why.
(Pause)
Because—no. I *don't* know why.
(Pause)
I thought I could start my life over again.
Which turned out not to be the case.
(Pause)
I didn't love him anymore.
I hadn't. For a long time...?
Then he got sick.

TATE: And you could've run.
But you didn't.

DUNN: I was trapped.

(Pause)

TATE: Why did you give me an alibi?

DUNN: I wanted someone to escape.

(Pause)

(TATE *passes* DUNN, *wading out into the water.*)

TATE: I am innocent—I swear.
But I'm also a liar. So who will believe me?

DUNN: What are you doing?

TATE: They train you—when you're in trouble—
to head for the water. Force of habit.
Go down the coast a ways, come ashore...
You can tell the police, when you saw me last,
I was heading out to sea.
No way I could survive.
Let me disappear.

(He's further out.)

TATE: Scatter his ashes, Mister Dunn.
You loved him. And he's gone.

(TATE *fades into the dark of the oncoming night.* DUNN
watches him go.)

(Then, almost unconsciously, he reaches into the urn.
He takes out a handful of ash, looks at it, lets it run through
his fingers.)

DUNN: I know. *(Pause)* Gone *where?*
(Pause)
Back. If we could go back...
If you could look up again, in the dark...
(He starts to scoop out handfuls of ash, and scatter them.)
If I could see your face...
(He scatters David's ashes.)

(The lights fade to black.)

END OF PLAY

CPSIA information can be obtained
at www.ICGtesting.com
Printed in the USA
BVHW042347020120
568131BV00012BA/352/P